ETCHED IN YOUR BRAIN NAME GAMES

FOR GROUPS OF ALL SIZES

MARTIN KEOGH

CONTENTS

Etched in Your Brain Name Games
Copyright: Martin Keogh ©2018
Publisher: Intimately Rooted Press
Paperback ISBN: 978-1-7752430-8-3
eBook ISBN: 978-1-7752430-9-0

Author photo: Nadja Meister

Find out more about the author and upcoming books at:
martinkeogh.com

INTRODUCTION

If you are a group leader of any kind – teacher, boss, camp counselor, professor, manager, group facilitator – then the enclosed games are for you. This book is also for those of us who simply have a hard time remembering which faces go with which names.

WHY AM I IN A POSITION TO WRITE THIS BOOK?

I have been a dance educator for over 38 years and have had the good fortune to teach in 32 countries spanning six continents. I also have four kids who have lots of friends.

I regularly work with groups of twenty to fifty people. Often, the group of students is completely new, both to me and to each other. At times, we have no one common language, which can become especially challenging when there are 10 or more nationalities in attendance.

I used to say, "I'm terrible at learning names," especially when the names are culturally foreign to my ear like Sanna Valkeapää, Eyal Vizner, and especially Nadezhda Kartaeva, where the accent lands on the fourth consonant.

However, because my profession demands that I regularly meet new people, I needed to come up with playful, easy ways to help me remember everyone. My students deserved this from me, and working as a group, they also deserved it from one another.

I found that combining fun activities with a dash of determination helps make learning names nearly effortless. When participants come up and say, "I can't believe I know everyone's name already," then we ALL can appreciate the bit of effort involved.

WHY SHOULD EVERYONE LEARN EACH OTHER'S NAMES?

- Names represent our individuality and allow us to recognize something intrinsically important in one another.
- Our names contain the complexities of our personal and cultural identity. They are how

we are recognized and summoned,
representing how we present ourselves.
- They are integral to how we constellate with
other people.

If I apply myself to learn my students' names, then I differentiate between them and distinguish them as individuals. I see each as a person and can more quickly offer individualized instruction. When the students recognize that I am seeing them as distinct individuals, they become more engaged in a supportive learning community.

When I call them by name, they feel seen and respected, and that respect and care gets transferred to how they treat one another. By this small action, my role as facilitator just became significantly easier.

As students learn each other's names and some personal details about each other's everyday lives, they can begin to feel more at ease. This leads to participants who are willing to ask more questions, take more risks, and bring more commitment and accountability to the group and the outcomes of the group.

I often start workshops by informing people that I'm terrible at remembering names. Those who also feel this way then respond with, "Oh, me too!" I follow up by saying, "but for this workshop (semester/seminar, etc.) let's all pretend we are experts at remembering names."

This is often followed by groans and laughter, and then we go on to actually learn everyone's name. Maybe not the first day, and maybe not the second, but by the end of our time together every one of us can look at each individual, recognize them, and speak their name.

WHAT WILL IT TAKE TO MAKE IT (NEARLY) EFFORTLESS? HERE ARE SEVEN TOOLS TO START WITH:

1. **Bite-size learning:** Accept you won't remember all of the names at once; instead allow yourself to remember a few at a time.
2. **Set the expectation** (softly)**:** Everyone will learn everyone else's name.
3. **Be repetitive**: Keep returning the group's focus to names.
4. **See the person when you hear their name:** Look at their face and body in detail.
5. **Get people up and active:** Moving people out of their chairs is a commitment to active learning. It also lets people associate the name with the face, body, and movement style of each individual.
6. **Enjoy the peculiarity of names:** If someone comes in with the name 'Ivy Sprout' or 'Swift Current,' they will be remembered because they stand out. Invite the same kind

of reaction to a Russian name like Xenia Myznikova. See if you can enjoy the sound and remember it for its distinctiveness.

7. *It's not about rote memorization. It's about seeing people and recognizing them by heart.*

WHAT WILL YOU FIND IN THIS BOOK?

- Intriguing topics for people to introduce themselves and each other to the group.
- Name games for sedentary professionals and name games for active and creative groups.
- A whole series of name games that get people in motion.
- 'Teachers' Tips for remembering names.
- Icons and an icon guide to find exercises that will work for *your* particular group.
- The raw material needed to come up with your own name games.

WHAT'S IN IT FOR YOU?

You are welcome to read this book from beginning to end or to open it up to a random page. This is about fun and effortlessness. Some people can learn thirty names in a day. For some, it's closer to ten or twenty, for others, forty. Use this book to find out how many you can learn *easily*. Even if you are good at remembering names, there will be people in your group who think that they can't. These games will have them learning with surprisingly little effort.

Like learning a new language, what helps most is simply aspiring to learn. Motivate yourself by understanding the value to you and your group. Then combine your desire and determination with the tools in this book. You and your groups will succeed without even knowing you are working at it.

ENJOY!

ICON GUIDE

Each name game in this book comes with a selection of icons.

These icons help you identify the name games that work best with your particular group.

The first icons will tell you what size group this name game works for. The second set of icons lets you know if the game is played sitting, standing or moving through the room.

SMALL SIZE GROUPS 4–11 PARTICIPANTS:

MEDIUM SIZE GROUPS 12–22 PARTICIPANTS:

LARGE SIZE GROUPS 23+ PARTICIPANTS:

OR SOME COMBINATION OF GROUP SIZE:

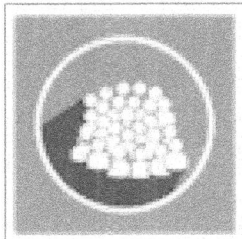

TYPES OF GAMES:

SITTING (ON THE FLOOR OR IN CHAIRS):

STANDING:

SITTING OR STANDING:

MOVING THROUGH THE ROOM:

ACTIVE NAME GAME: (NEEDS A PHYSICAL WARM-UP)

COZY GROUPS: (FOR GROUPS COMFORTABLE WITH
MORE INTIMACY AND PLAYFULNESS)

CHAPTER 1

ONE NAME AT A TIME

BEFORE WE LEAP into the name games below is what could be the most valuable tool for learning names.

In Moonwalking with Einstein: The Art and Science of Remembering Everything, Joshua Foer reports the reasons that using visualizations works so well when remembering names. Psychologists have named this kind of memorization the "Baker/baker paradox." A researcher shows a photograph of a man to a group of people. Half of the group is told that the man's name is Baker. The other half of the group is told that the man's profession is being a baker. A couple of days later, the groups are shown the photo again. The group that was told the man's profession is much more likely to remember than the group that was told the name.

A name like Baker just hangs in space with no connections to draw it up in our memory. However, we have many multi-sensory associations with the profession of 'baker.' We have various ways to recall memories, from the smell of fresh bread to the white apron, and even to our love for certain breads or pastries. *When you hear that the man is a baker, you embed the word in an entire network of ideas and senses you already hold.*

When we hear a name, we are more likely to remember it if we create a visualization that anchors that name in the same part of the brain as *"baker."* Our job is to make a habit of creating a visual image for each person we meet. The more weird or fierce the image, the better. For "Dylan," picture a dill pickle: for "Barbara," a barbed-wire fence; for "Sophie," a soft-freeze ice cream.

It also helps if we can apply the image to some detail about the person or some detail about where we met. For instance, if you meet "Ray" on a sunny beach you can picture sun "rays" shooting out of his head.

Some names are easy because the image is inherent in the name. Names like Jack, Robin, Jasmine, and Matt are already images. The next set of names are easily turned into images because they rhyme: Laura: fedora or Madelyn: violin. And some names you add your imagination to for the image: Hazel: becomes a witch over her cauldron: witch hazel. Or with the name Noah: Noah's ark (filling with animals two by two).

Here are fifteen more examples (more detailed images are in the parenthesis):

Name	Image:
• Aaron:	Going for 'A" run
• Abigail:	A bagel (with oozing cream cheese)
• Alecia:	Putting a leash on the dog (favorite breed)
• Alexa:	A Lexus (add your favorite model)
• Anar:	An "R" (on an oversized billboard)
• Barbara:	A barber (in front of the striped barber pole)
• Bill:	Billions of stars in the milky way
• Bob:	Bobbing for apples (dressed for Halloween)
• Bradshaw	Bad ass with a chainsaw (slicing a "B" in a tree)
• Chase:	Police chasing a thief
• Claire:	Cat caught in a 'snare'
• Cole:	Has a big black mole (on his chin)
• Debora:	"D cup" bra
• Frank:	100% beef frank hot dog (with mustard)
• Grace:	Shooting mace (in the face)

Making a habit of adding images to names when you first meet people is the best way to build your skill of remembering people. You can start by creating the image as soon as the person departs. As you get more skilled, you will come up with the image the moment you hear the name.

Now it's your turn to practice. Below are fifteen names. Try creating an image to go with each name. Have fun; go hog wild; create the craziest images you can. Those are the ones you can't forget.

Name
• Heidi
• Jacob
• Jay
• Lisa
• Lynn
• Martinez
• Max
• Mike
• Mitchell
• Nicole
• Oscar
• Paige
• Sherri
• Victoria

Come up with your own images before turning the page. On the next page are the names with images attached.

Name	Image:
• Heidi:	Playing hide and go seek
• Jacob:	Holding a Jaguar cub
• Jay:	Jay walking on a busy street
• Lisa:	The Mona Lisa's smile
• Lynn:	Lint (all over the blanket)
• Martinez:	Salt rimmed martini
• Max:	This person in cli-max
• Mike:	A large microphone
• Mitchell:	A baseball mitt catching a shell (mitt-shell)
• Nicole:	Pole dancer (flipping upside down on the pole)
• Oscar:	A scar (across the face)
• Paige:	Page of a cookbook
• Sherri:	A spilled glass of sherry (on a white carpet)
• Victoria:	The team runs up to the fans yelling "Victory!"

CHAPTER 2

TEACHER MEMORY TIPS

21 TIPS FOR REMEMBERING NAMES:

1. If you see someone and don't remember their name, try reintroducing yourself. Nine times out of ten, the person will respond by telling you their name.
2. Don't be afraid to ask someone's name – you might say "I know YOU, but I don't have your name yet – please tell me again." Or simply, "Tell me your name again."
3. Repetition: Use the names you have just learned as often as you can. "It's a pleasure to meet you, Maria."
4. Make it a personal project to greet each person individually before your class or event gets started. Tell them your name and ask for theirs. You can also ask if you have met before

and where. Carry a notebook and write the name down, adding some description (especially about their hair, or particularities of their face – scars, piercings, the color of their eyes).

5. With your attendance list use codes next to people's names. Notice some physical trait and create your own symbols: dots if they have freckles or pimples; glasses if they have eyeglasses; if they are tall put 2 vertical lines; a big circle if they are round-bodied; a halo for bald heads; hair over the name for long hair, etc.

6. While participants are involved in some activity, take out the name list and underline the names you know already.

7. Between meetings review the list.

8. Accept that you won't remember everyone's names all at once. Simply remember a few at a time.

9. If a person has a hard to pronounce name ask them for a way to help you remember it. Many people are used to their names being mangled and already have some memory trick up their sleeves. They will appreciate you asking.

10. Asking is almost always helpful. Chinese names have the surname first and the given name second. It's OK to ask which first name the person goes by.

11. Ask the person where the name comes from. Often the story will help the name stick.

12. Ask students to photocopy their ID cards for you. Use these as flashcards to learn all the names.

13. Better yet, have participants make you a "passport" with a passport photo and details about themselves.

14. Provide index cards for people to make nametags. Have everyone pass the cards back to you at the end of class; your task is to pass them back correctly at the next meeting.

15. To help everyone with names, post a names list on the wall along with everyone's photo.

16. Learn to take pride in learning the trills and accents of names that are in languages foreign to you.

17. Make a joke about forgetting names: "Some days I can't even remember my own name."

18. People are flattered when you remember their names. Learn to enjoy gratifying people in this way.

19. At the end of a name game, go around and say each person's name. People will be surprised that you can do it and it will give everyone the incentive to learn themselves.

20. Along with the visualization you create for each name, immediately associate the name with some detail you already know about the person, "Margarita (A SALT-RIMMED

MARGARITA GLASS) from Colorado,"
"Barry (BARE NAKED BEAR) who used to
run the deli."

21. It can't be said enough: to help you and all the
participants learn all the names, get up and
get moving! Move around as you learn.

CHAPTER 3

IN MOTION: DROP-DEAD GORGEOUS NAME GAMES

THERE ARE no lack of name games and variations in this book. To make it easy for you I'm starting with the most effective ones. While there are lots of games that people can do sitting or standing in a circle (see chapters five to eight), I cannot recommend enough that you get people moving around the room. Here's why:

While the brain is only two percent of our body's mass, it uses up a fifth of all the oxygen we breath and a quarter of all the glucose we consume. To get our brains activated into laying down new memories, it helps to engage the entire body.

Remembering names easily comes down to three basic ground rules:

1. Keep coming back to people's names: repetition
2. Attach wild images to each person's name

3. Get people in motion

Having fun does help!

Please note that this icon connotes name games for groups that are comfortable with more playfulness and closeness:

The name games where people need a physical warm-up have this icon:

Let the Games Begin

HANDSHAKES

Set up:

Explain the game and send people on a stroll around the room.

Instructions:

Step One: Have people walk around, shake hands and say their names.

Step Two: The facilitator calls out a new body part like "elbows." Then, rather than shake hands, they shake elbows instead. You can call out: knees, backs, butts, noses, etc.

Variation:

The facilitator calls out some other task like to bow, do a waltz, or skip around each other.

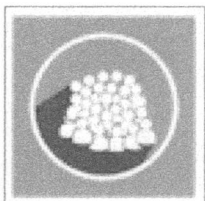

GLUE HANDSHAKES

Set up:

Explain the game and send people on a stroll around the room.

Instructions:

Step One: Shake hands with people and introduce yourself.

Step Two: Same as above, but you can't let go of one person's hand until you are shaking another person's hand.

I AM A PERSON WHO...

Set up:

Explain the game and send people on a stroll around the room.

Instructions:

Walk around and meet someone. Each says their name and then says "I am a person who..." Each time they say this sentence they must complete it with a different detail about themselves that is true.

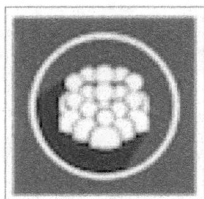

Variation:

Have everyone make up things that are not true.

Variation for cozier groups:

After you have done this exercise for a while, have everyone pause and think about a detail from their life that is more revealing, personal, even risqué. In one turn everyone speaks their detail. From then on you always repeat the detail you just heard as if it were your own. This is hilarious when your detail comes back to you changed. (**For this to work the group has to understand that they always repeat the detail they most recently heard!**)

SUFI SHOULDER GREETING

Set up:

Demonstrate and then send people on a stroll around the room.

Instructions:

Two people walk toward each other, arms outstretched. They each place both of their hands on the others left shoulder, cradling it. They each say their own name. They then begin to step back, allowing their hands to slide down the others arm, right to the finger-tips. They then repeat this action on the right arm starting with both hands on the shoulder. This time they ay their partner's name.

NAME GAUNTLET

Set up:

The group stands in two lines facing each other about three feet apart. Each line stands shoulder to shoulder.

Instructions:

A person from the end of one of the lines stands at the head of the gauntlet and says their name. They then walk down the gauntlet as everyone repeatedly whispers their name back to them.

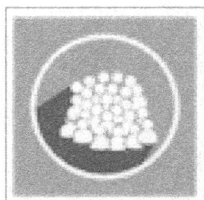

At the end of the gauntlet the person turns to be seen by everyone and then their name is said aloud. The person thanks the group and joins the end of the line.

SCAVENGER HUNT

Set up:

Explain and send people on a stroll through the room. Have "trait sheets" with blank lines next to each trait, for everyone. The trait sheets have lists of general traits like: I eat midnight snacks; I'm an early riser; etc.

Instructions:

Give each person a trait sheet. They walk around and find a person that has one of the traits and that person signs their name on the trait sheet. A person's name cannot show up more than once on any given sheet.

Variation:

Have some of the traits relate directly to what your group is working on.

WHO'S BEHIND THE BLANKET?

Set up:

Split the group into two teams and have them sit on the floor or in chairs facing each other. Two people hold up a blanket between the groups so the teams cannot see each other.

Instructions:

One person from each team sits in front of the blanket, but on their team's side. The people holding the blanket count to three then drop it. The newly revealed people facing each other race to say the other person's name. Whoever says the name first wins and the loser goes to the winning team. Repeat.

TRIED AND TRUE NAME GAME

Thanks to Clover Catskill for so many variations on this one.

Set up:

Have everyone stand in a circle.

Instructions:

A person says their name and makes a physical motion/movement. The group repeats the name and motion back (when introducing the game recommend to the group that the movements be easy to mimic).

Variation #1:

You can do this game sequentially around the circle or have people go when they are ready.

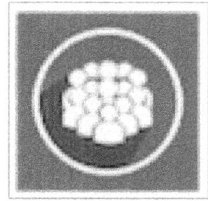

Variation #2:

Repeat the name and motion three times.

Variation #3:

Each time someone says a name and does a motion, the group repeats that one and then all the others done thus far. (For groups of under 20.)

THE YES CIRCLE

Thanks to Aaron Brando for contributing this game. This is an exercise that helps set the tone for focusing, following directions, and synchronizing as a group. It can be played on the first day of being together and repeated throughout.

Set up:

Start in a standing circle.

Instructions:

Step One: One person begins by looking around the circle. When they make eye contact with someone in the circle, they say that person's name. That person simply replies with "yes", and finds someone else in the circle to make eye contact with, then says their name. This continues until the class finds a rhythm together.

Step Two: After a person receives the "yes" they walk over and take that spot in the circle (as if the unspoken request is "may I take your spot?"). During the time the asker is walking, the person who gave the "yes" finds another person in the circle, says their name and walks towards the new spot. Again, this continues until the class finds a rhythm together.

Variation:

Rather than saying the person's name in order to receive the "yes," this round is played by only using eye contact to communicate.

NAME JAM

Thanks to Rick Nodine for this contribution.

Set up:

Have everyone sit in a circle on the floor. Save this one for a day when the group has had some experience with each other.

Instructions:

Step One: Going around the circle, each person says all the names that have come before them in the circle and finishes with their own name. The last person (the teacher) then says all the names in the circle.

Step Two: One person gets up from where they are sitting in the circle, moves somewhere new in the space and describes what they are doing in relation to another person. They must use the persons name in their description. For example: "I am sitting behind Jane." "I am looking into the eyes of Donatella." The person who is named in the statement must go off and do the same in another place with another person.

Step Three: You can then encourage people to do actions that include more than one person. For example: "I am lying at the feet of Daniel, Jonna, and Mike." This causes the activity in the room to multiply and usually leads to lots of laughter.

BEST NAME GAME EVER

This is the most effective name game I've come across. It is fun, and builds group cohesion and enlivens people for whatever is to come. Visual learners, auditory learners, and kinesthetic learners are all addressed.

Special thanks to the dance teachers Benno Vorheim and Scott Wells who taught me many variations.

Set up:

Have the group stand in a circle but not touching. Use a soft ball about 10" in diameter. Foam balls work well, as do small pillows. My favorites are 'Overballs' from Italy because they are soft, easy to catch, and deflate for easy transporting. Even people who are uncomfortable with ball games soon become confident with these.

Instructions:

Step One: Start with one ball. The person with the ball meets somebody's eyes and throws the ball to them. The catcher then says their name. This continues until everybody's name has been heard at least once. The ball is always thrown underhand with a high arc, so it is easy to catch. No overhand throwing unless the group gets really good at this.

Step Two: Catching eyes, the thrower says the intended catcher's name first, and then throws the ball.

Step Three: Add balls one at a time, up to five. This can get quite energetic and uproarious.

Variation #1:

Every so often stop the action and say, "Everyone walk through the middle and find a new place in the circle." This encourages people to actually learn the names and not just hang the names in the space where the person was standing.

Variation #2:

When someone thinks they know all the names they can try to say them.

Variation #3:

One person in the center of the circle. They say someone's name and throw the ball straight up. The new person has to run in and catch the ball as the first person returns to the outer circle.

Variation #4:

Same as above, but as the person catches the ball they fall to the floor. (This one needs participants to be quite physically warmed-up.)

Variation #5:

After doing this in a circle, have everyone walk through the room. The person with the ball says a name, catches the eyes of that person and then throws the ball underhand to them.

Variation #6:

Same as above, but to raise the energy, people can steal the ball from the receiver. Tell people they can't steal the ball from the person throwing the ball, they can only steal it when near the person who is trying to catch it. (This one needs people to be quite physically warmed-up)

Variation #7–99:

This name game is rich for improvisation. Come up with your own variations and send them to me!

GAMES FOR MORE COZY GROUPS

HUG NAMES

Set up:

Explain and send people on a stroll through the room.

Instructions:

Step One: Have people give each other A-frame hugs, embracing around the shoulders and keeping their hips apart. Before they enter the hug they say their own names. As they leave the hug they say their partner's name.

Step Two: Have people walk around at their tallest height, on tip-toes even, and give people hugs (these will be somewhat stiff hugs.)

Step Three: Have people walk around about 2 centimeters shorter than their full height. Then hug and pour or mold into each other. You can see why this game needs a group of people willing to be close.

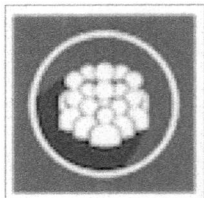

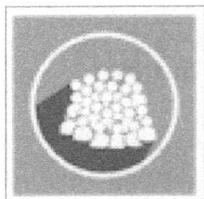

BACK OF HAND KISSES

Set up:

Demonstrate and then send people on a stroll around the room.

Instructions:

Walk around and lift your hand in front of your face, then grasp the hand of your partner. Turn the back of

their hand to your face so that you both kiss the back of your partner's hand at the same time. Beforehand they say their own names. As they depart, but while still close, they say their partner's name.

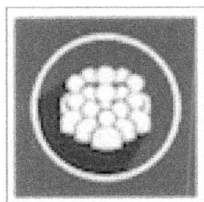

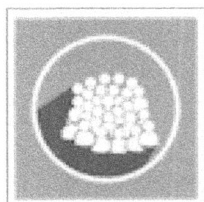

CHAPTER 4

FEISTY NAME GAMES

The following games need a thorough physical
warm-up to be effective AND safe.

STEALING PLACES

SET UP:

Start by standing in a tighter circle
where each person is almost
touching the person to either side.

Instructions:

Step One: Tell people they have to remember at least one new name and then go around and have each person say their name. Then anyone can call out someone's name and the two have to exchange places in the circle.

Step Two: Put one or two people in the middle of the circle. Everyone else stands touching almost shoulder to shoulder. When someone calls a name and those people are exchanging places, one of the people in the circle can steal one of the two empty places, leaving a new person stuck in the middle. It's good to tell the group: "Imagine that you are like cotton candy: big and colorful but without mass. This way there are no collisions."

Variation: Remove the saying of names and have people exchange places when they meet each other's eyes.

CATCH ME

Set up:

Explain and send people on a stroll around the room.

Instructions:

Call out your name and then put your arms in the air above your head. Rigid like a board, slowly begin to fall. Two or three people have to run over to catch you and set you back to walking.

Variation:

The catchers (or the entire room) say the fallers name repeatedly as they put the faller back on to their center.

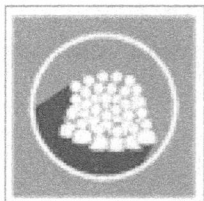

GRAVITY NAMES

Set up:

Space everyone out around the room at least a few meters apart

Instructions:

The facilitator has a list of names. She calls out a name and that person throws their arms in the air. Everyone runs to tag that person. They then return to being equidistant.

Variation #1:

The person who was just named then names the next person.

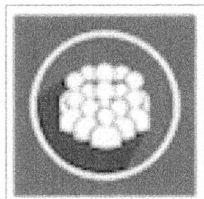

Variation #2:

Rather than standing static, this can be done as people walk through the room.

NAME TAG

Thanks to the master of games, Brad Stoller, for this variation.

Set up:

Demonstrate and then send people on a stroll around the room.

Instructions:

If you are about to be tagged, you can call out someone's name. That person is now the one who is "it." For safety tell people to walk fast and not run.

Variation:

Raise the stakes by having a person who gets tagged be "out": they then stand at the side. If someone calls

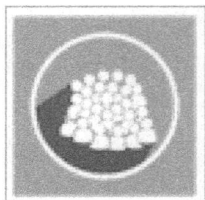

out the name of someone who is already out, then they are also out.

CHAPTER 5

MESMERIZING NAME GAMES

Games for sitting in chairs or on the floor.
Some of these can also be done standing.

PRIOR NAMES

Set up:

Have everyone sit in a circle.

Instructions:

Step One: Go around the circle counter-clockwise. Each person says the name of the person to their left and then their own name.

Step Two: Repeat, saying the two prior names, then three, etc.

Variation:

In groups of 15 or less, keep adding names until each person introduces every other person in the circle. People can help those who get stuck.

FERAL IMAGES, FIERCE IMPRESSIONS

Set up:

Have everyone sit in a circle.

Instructions:

The group comes up with an image for each participant that fits the person's name. The wilder the image, the easier it will be to remember the name. For "Dennis" see a dentist drilling a tooth. For "Liana," see her peeling a banana. For "Dillon" see a villain in a black cape in the wind. For "Nicolette," see a marionette with wild jerky movements.

Variation:

Once you have come up with images for everyone, go around and have each person say the image that the group came up with. Then the group says the name.

Special thanks to Carol Swann for this name game.

Set up:

Have everyone sit or stand in a circle.

Instructions:

The first person starts by saying, "My name is Carol and I have an itch here" (I put a finger on my nose). The next person says, "Her name is Carol and she has an itch here (puts finger on own nose) and my name is Federico and I have an itch here (puts finger on knee or wherever they want"). You continue around the circle adding each person in.

Variation #1:

Rather than "I have an itch here" use "I like to be touched here"

Variation #2:

"I'm ticklish here."

Variation #3:

"I have an erogenous zone here."

Variation #4:

"Never touch me here."

MY... NAME... IS...

Set up:

Have everyone sit or stand in a circle.

Instructions:

Each person simply says their name.

Variations

When people say their names in a circle they often speed up. When this happens, the group doesn't have the time to associate the name with the person. Some ways to keep the pace steady are:

Variation #1:

Say the name, look at the eye color of the next person, then that person says their name.

Variation #2:

Take a breath and say your name.

Variation #3:

Say your name and make a gesture with your hands.

Variation #4:

Say your name and make a movement with your body.

CLAP NAMES

Thanks to Anne Aronov for contributing this game.

Set up:

Have everyone sit or stand in a circle.

Instructions:

Leader says their name with a clap. They then look to their right, meet their neighbor's eyes, and they both clap and say the name. Then, the entire group says the name with a clap. Then person #2 starts the sequence again. The key is to clap and to make eye contact with each name.

Variation:

When the entire group says the name, they then clap and say every name that has gone before in reverse order.

NAME RITUAL

Set up:

Have everyone stand in a circle.

Instructions:

Person steps forward and says, "My name is Barbara." The group responds with, "Your name is Barbara! Barbara! Barbara!" The person thanks the group and returns to the circle.

Variation:

When the group says the name back, they speak in a whisper the first time, a normal voice the second, and heartily the third time.

NAME MEDITATION

Set up:

Have everyone sit in a circle.

Instructions:

Someone says their name and then people meditate on the person's face and name.

Variation:

A person stands up so that people can meditate on their face and entire body.

NAME TOSS

Set up:

Have everyone sit or stand in a circle.

Instructions:

Say your name to the person next to you. That person repeats your name and then turns and says their name to the next person. Let this speed up.

Variation:

Slow it back down, and when someone repeats a name they can then send their name to someone across the circle. The person across the circle repeats the name and can then send their own name to either side or send their name to a new person across the circle.

WRITTEN NAMES

This one takes some time.

Set up:

Demonstrate, and then have half of the group sit on the floor or in chairs while the other half walks around.

Instructions:

The sitting people close their eyes. The walking people walk up and each one stands behind someone. With a finger, they write their name one letter at a time on the person's back in big block letters. The sitting person tries to guess the name. Do this many times and then switch who is sitting and who is walking.

"BATIZADO MINEIRO"

This game comes from my friend Fernando Neder in Rio de Janeiro, Brazil.

He says, "This is one of my favorites. I call it 'Batizado Mineiro.' In Portuguese "Batizado" means to baptize or to name. "Mineiro" refers to someone who was born in the Brazilian state of Minas Gerais. People from that region are known for, among other things, being reserved. So, the game helps us to introduce ourselves in a fun way. It works very well with shy groups to "break the ice." This game is even good for large groups. Musical learners will memorize by the sound. Kinesthetic learners will remember through the movement."

Set up:

Have everyone sit or stand in a circle.

Instructions:

Step One: Go around, each person says their name and the group echoes the name back.

Step Two: Each person says their name and a word that starts with the same letter. For example: Fernando / faith. The group repeats the name and word with the same rhythm, same melody, same intensity, etc.

Step Three: Name / same word / and a movement expressing that word (in Fernando's case, for instance, he would hold his hands together in front of his chest like he was praying). The group repeats everything, including the movement.

Step Four: The person only does the word and movement. The group repeats.

Step Five: The person does only the movement. The group does the movement, the word, AND the name.

BALL OF YARN

Set up:

Have everyone sit in a circle on the floor. Have a ball of colorful yarn.

Instructions:

The facilitator says their name and an interesting detail about themselves. (Let people come up with their own details or use one of the topics from Chapter #7.) The facilitator then holds the end of the yarn and rolls or throws the ball to someone. That person then says the previous person's name and detail, followed by their name and a detail from their life. They then roll or throw the yarn and this continues until every name and detail is repeated.

By the end, everyone sees that they are connected in a big web.

Variation #1:

Roll the yarn back up by saying the name and detail of the person you received the yarn from.

Variation #2:

Say the name and detail of every single person before you and then your own.

Variation #3:

This one is for a group that already has information about each other. The person holding the yarn says their name and then the name and detail of the person they are going to throw the yarn to. "My name is Ricki and I'm throwing the yarn to Mascha because I remember that Mascha likes double-fudge chocolate ice-cream."

CHAPTER 6

INDELIBLE INTRODUCTIONS

PEOPLE ARE INTERESTING. Many have fascinating stories, and many have the imagination to make up interesting tales about themselves. Below are a series of introduction games for people to introduce themselves. This evolves to learning a detail about a partner and then introducing their partner to the group.

One of the tricks to learning names is to associate the sound of a person's name with details you can clearly imagine. By weaving the name with strong, vivid images, it helps bring the name back when needed.

The more senses we use, the more we can relate to the name of the person, the more hooks will embed into the network of what our memory holds about that person.

You can take this one step further. Our brains have

evolved to be especially interested in sex and jokes. Particularly jokes about sex! If we want to really be remembered, we will introduce ourselves with funny, wacky, or bawdy stories. So, if appropriate with your group, use the more bizarre introduction topics from the list below.

Most of these introduction exercises are done sitting in a circle on the floor or in chairs:

Some can be done standing:

Or you can choose either:

Introductions work best with small to medium size groups:

INTRODUCING YOURSELF

SLOW MOTION INTRODUCTION

In this time of increasing cultural exchange, we some-times find ourselves in rooms filled with people whose names are not native to each other's ears. This intro-duction exercise is especially useful when there are challenging names in the mix.

Instructions:

Say your name in very slow motion. Exaggerate every vowel and consonant.

Variation:

This one facilitates memory because of the repetition. Say "my name is..." in a normal voice followed with the name in exaggerated slow motion. Then say it in normal speed. Then say it in a fast high-pitched voice. Then back to normal speed.

FAME NAME

Instructions:

Each person thinks of an adjective that has the same

first letter as their name: "I'm Mellow Martin" or "I'm Beautiful Beatrice."

Variation #1:

Use a rhyming word: "I'm Fairy Mary" or "I'm Hairy Mary."

Variation #2:

Create an entire sentence with most of the first letters being the same: "I'm freaky Fred, I like following football." One possible pattern is: I'm (adjective)-(name). I like (action-ing)-(noun).

Variation #3:

Say your name and then use the first letter of your name to be the first letter of a food: "I'm Angela anchovies" or "I'm Benno banana."

Variation #4:

With any of the above variations, each person says all that came before and then their own.

WHISPER NAMES

Set up:

This one can be done sitting but is better done standing in a circle.

Instructions:

Each person whispers their name, then says it in a normal voice to the group, and then at full volume to the horizon. For full volume ask people to "make the windows shake."

IMAGE AND NAME

Instructions:

Add an image to the name. Say the entire image and then take one word away at a time until you just hear the name.

Example: Michelle strong mountain! / Michelle strong! / Michelle!

INTRODUCING YOUR PARTNER

COMMONALITIES

Instructions:

Give each pair two minutes to find five things they have in common. Together, they introduce each other with their commonalities.

Variation:

Find five things that are different about each other.

FAMOUS.SHAMOUS

Instructions:

Introduce the person to your right. With incredible imagination and hyperbole, invent a character where the only true fact is the person's name (which, of course should be repeated regularly).

Example: "I'm extremely honored that we have in our midst, Mary Ford, the first person to break the sound barrier while bungee jumping. Mary spent 13 years of her life in a cave with Tibetan monks, and since coming down has invented the "chi machine," a device that turns gold into chocolate. I'm very pleased to present to you, Mary Ford."

Variation:

Each introduction uses one detail and the name from the previous introduction and then exceeds that detail.

Example: "While Mary Ford might have invented the device that turns gold into chocolate, and Mary might have been quite proud of this, it is nothing compared to Samuel Evans. Samuel Evans, through decades of cross-breeding, has come up with the Juniper bush that blooms one-hundred-dollar bills. As you might imagine people are often yelling Samuel, oh Samuel, be my friend!"

CHAPTER 7

UNFORGETTABLE INTRODUCTION TOPICS

FOR INTRODUCING YOUR PARTNER OR YOURSELF

A MAJOR WAY TO learn names is to have people introduce themselves or someone else to the group.

To set up partner introductions, split the group into pairs. Each person interviews their partner to find out some detail(s) that they will later use to introduce this person to the entire group.

You can invite people to spend ten minutes or more in the interview to find out many details or you can save time by giving one or two of the topics below.

The great value of this partner exercise is that people are less inhibited when introducing someone else. They feel less self-conscious and they get used to feeling more at ease in the group, which helps with group cohesion.

Feel free to invent topics close to your field or invent

topics that address what your group is working with on any given day.

Have people say the name of their partner or themselves at LEAST three times during the introduction. It can help if you go first to model this and also to set the rhythm.

These topics can also be used for people introducing themselves.

These are mostly done sitting in chairs or on the floor.

Some of these topics require comfort with candor. Decide which are appropriate for your particular group.

Use with small to medium size groups.

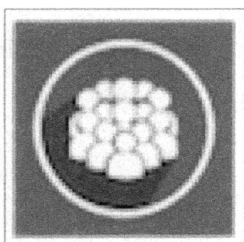

SIMPLE TOPICS:

- Favorite thing about summer
- Something that makes you calm
- Name and breed of a childhood pet
- Favorite piece of clothing and why
- Where you were born
- If you could be an animal for a day, what animal would it be?
- Most prized possession
- Something you've done that we haven't

- A goal you want to accomplish in this lifetime
- The superhero you would like to be
- The superpower you would like to have
- The actor you would choose to play YOU in the movie about your life

FOOD:

- Favorite cuisine (in detail)
- Childhood comfort food
- The most delicious food you've ever eaten
- What food from home you miss
- What food from home you don't miss

TELL US A BRIEF STORY:

- A proudest moment
- One of your pet peeves
- An unusual detail about yourself
- Tell us about one time when you were happy
- A scary experience
- A lie you've told
- The first place and time you would visit if you had a time machine
- A story about where your name came from or how you received it
- Show us and tell us the story of one of your scars

- Tell us one detail about yourself that is not true
- An award you would like to win and for what achievement
- Tell us something that you hate and something that you love
- Name an organization or person you would support if you were a philanthropist
- Say your name, where you are from, and a fact or fiction about yourself

TODAY'S TOPICS:

- Tell us what brought you here
- Tell us what you imagine your role is in this group
- Speak of the worst project you were part of
- Name something that could bring this group closer
- Tell us what your ideal class / workshop / course would consist of

TOPICS THAT INVITE MORE CANDOR:

- Closest you've been to death
- Closest you've been to life
- Tell us about something you desire
- The biggest question on your mind right now

- A time you broke the law or a rule
- Tell us a sensual detail about yourself
- Show us one of your favorite sleeping positions
- Show us a body part you particularly like today
- Where were you conceived?
- What is something unfinished about you?

SIXTY QUESTIONS FOR INTRODUCTIONS

Everyone can answer the same question, or you can give each person a different question.

You will find variations of these in the chapter of sentence completions.

1. As a child, did you ever plan to, pack for, or actually run away from home?
2. If you have a pet, how did you decide on its name?
3. If your neighbor's dog routinely kept you awake at night, what would you do?
4. What would be an ideal dream job for you?
5. If you won the lottery what would you change in your life?
6. What is one embarrassing moment in your life?

7. What's one of the foolhardy things you did as a kid?

8. What's one of the foolhardy things you did as an adult?

9. Did you ever go to a restaurant and walk out on the bill?

10. What sport do you love to watch, but would never try yourself?

11. If you died and you could come back as anyone who would it be? Why?

12. If you could live anywhere in the world, where would you live and why?

13. What is an endearing thing your child/spouse/parent/dear friend does that warms your heart?

14. Name one neighbor (or coworker) who has been especially kind or supportive to you this year.

15. What are the first three things you can name that you are grateful for?

16. Who is the person who has had the most influence on your choice of career?

17. If you had a chance to invite two famous people to dinner in your home, whom would you choose? Why?

18. What trade that used to be essential in medieval society – that is no longer practiced – would you like to apprentice for? (cobbler, wheelwright, miller, etc.)

19. What is your favorite piece of technology?

20. What is the most annoying thing about today's technology?

21. What was your favorite subject in school? In college?

22. Name one class or subject area that you avoided in school/college. Why?

23. How did you pick the name/s of your child/ren?

24. What is one of your pet peeves?

25. In detail, what is your favorite food?

26. Which animal intrigues you? Why?

27. Is there an animal species that makes you uncomfortable? Why?

28. What is a favorite memory of one of your childhood best friends?

29. Who was your favorite teacher in school, and why?

30. Were you ever sweet on one of your teachers?

31. If your parent(s) were here, what would they say was the most challenging part of raising you?

32. What's the boldest thing anyone ever dared you to do? Did you do it?

33. Do you remember the first time your parents really lost it because of something you did?

34. What was your favorite neighborhood play/pastime as a kid?

35. If you could go back and be any age you wanted, what age would you choose?

36. When did you get your first car? Was it a clunker?

37. How did you and your spouse/partner meet?

38. If you knew you would be spending a couple of hours in a waiting room, what would you take with you to keep you busy?

39. Do you consider yourself a follower or a leader?

40. When you are trying to find a space in a crowded parking lot, are you a hawk or a lamb?

41. If you could go back and live in another part of history, which period would you choose?

42. Name one thing you discovered about one of your family members that took you by surprise?

43. Do you have a tattoo? If not, what design would you consider?

44. What is the most unusual thing that you carry in your purse/backpack/briefcase?

45. What is one of your quirks?

46. Can you name a personal quirk that even your closest friends might not know about you?

47. Name the oddest quirk you can think of in a spouse, friend, neighbor, etc.

48. Is there anything that you are OCD (obsessive compulsive) about?

49. When you brush your teeth, do you roll the

tube up from the bottom, or do you just
squeeze wherever?

50. What is your morning ritual?

51. If you could reinvent yourself, what new
identity or lifestyle or career choice would
you choose?

52. If your pet could speak, what would he say
about you?

53. What time of day do you do your best work?

54. Name one thing you like about your own
appearance.

55. Name one positive character trait that you
believe defines you.

56. When you cook, do you follow a recipe, or do
you improvise?

57. Are you first born, somewhere in the middle,
the youngest, or an only child?

58. What was your first career dream? How old
were you?

59. What do you do to stay in shape?

60. What do you most enjoy doing when you
want to unwind at the end of the day?

CHAPTER 8

ETCHED IN YOUR BRAIN: SENTENCE COMPLETIONS

ASK EACH PERSON TO begin with: "My name is..." and then to complete one of the sentence completions below.

Example: "My name is Michelle. The riskiest thing I've ever done was to cross a border by hiking through the mountains."

Everyone can use the same sentence completion, or you can toss a different one to each person.

Use the sentence completions below or formulate new ones that make sense for the goals or personality of your group. Some of the sentence completions below ask for candor. Know which ones will work for your particular dynamic. These can generate a wonderful edge to your group's interaction but be mindful of overstepping people's boundaries. Sentence completions allow you to entice beneficial information while having the group effortlessly learn names.

Below are some sample sentence completions. Mix, choose, and create new ones as you please.

SIMPLE:

- Three words that describe me are...
- One of the most soothing sounds for me is...
- The actor I would like to play the role of me is...
- I love the scent of...
- One of my favorite animals is...
- One of my favorite books is...
- I waste time by...
- If I could go anywhere in the world, I'd go to...
- When I was a child I thought I would grow up to be a...
- I can't get enough of...
- I am proud of my...
- When I die, the animal I would like to come back as is a...
- A favorite piece of technology is...

- When I want to unwind at the end of the day, I enjoy...
- If I could go back 5 years and thank someone, it would be...
- Last weekend, I...

EATING:

- The strangest thing I've ever eaten was...
- I would never eat...
- A favorite dish is...
- I like the texture in my mouth of...
- If I could have a dessert as the main course, it would be...
- When I'm really hungry my favorite emergency meal is...
- A weird food combination that I love is...

TALKING:

- I enjoy discussing...
- I dislike discussing...
- One of the best times I've spent in conversation was...
- Talking about relationship issues makes me...
- Whispering in my ear makes me...
- Singing to me makes me...

BODY:

- One thing I like about my appearance is...
- One thing I would change about how I look is...
- When I'm nude I feel...
- I enjoy how my body feels when I...

SPORTS/EXERCISE:

- My favorite way to exercise is...
- My favorite team sport to watch is...
- My favorite individual sport to watch is...
- My favorite team sport to participate in is...
- My favorite individual sport to participate in is...
- If I had unlimited time for working out, I'd...
- The dumbest sport in the world is...

EDUCATION:

- I wish I'd learned how to...
- Even if it kills me, I'll learn how to...
- In college I majored in (will major in)...
- If I could make a living at it, I'd have learned...

- My favorite subject in school was...
- One class or subject area that I avoided like the plague in school was...
- My greatest strength as a student is...

THE FUTURE:

- When I grow up I want to be...
- In the next month I will...
- In the next year I will...
- In five years, I hope I've accomplished...
- I will consider my life well-lived if I can...
- I will consider my life wasted if I don't...
- The number of kids I'd like is...
- In five years, my livelihood will be...
- In twenty-five years, I hope I...
- In fifty years I see myself...
- Before I die, I want to...
- If I had a year to live, I would...
- If I won the lottery I would...

REVEALING:

- Some good advice I received was...
- Some bad advice I received was...
- The most important decision I ever made was...
- My earliest memory is...

- The best thing that ever happened to me was...
- I am better than anyone at...
- The one thing I routinely do when driving, which I would be too embarrassed to do if I had a passenger is...
- A positive character trait that helps define me is that I am...
- I am grateful for...
- One of the riskiest things I ever did was...
- The most foolhardy thing I've ever done was...
- If I could throw caution to the wind and really risk, I would...
- An embarrassing moment was when I...
- One type of pain that I like to feel is the pain of...
- My top three ways to handle stress are...
- The first person in my life who died was...
- If I could go back in time and change one thing I would...
- If I could change one thing about myself it would be...
- One of my regrets is...
- My last relationship ended because...
- The thing I desire most in a partner is...
- I believe lovemaking should be...
- A moment that helped define me was...

MORE REVELATION:

- I feel butterflies in my stomach when...
- I'm happy when...
- I'm sad when...
- I cry when...
- When I am alone, I feel...
- When I am with a large group of people, I feel...
- To break the ice, I usually...
- I feel awkward when...
- A high point in my life was when...
- A felt proud when...
- Within the last 48 hours, the best moment for me was...
- My favorite old road or street to drive down or walk down is...
- The last time I felt unbounded enthusiasm was...
- An example of when I was shocked was...
- A time when I was absolutely outraged was when...
- I feel cranky when...
- I feel tranquil when...

FAMILY:

- In my family I was born (birth order)...

- My ancestry is...
- As a child, I was generally...
- In my family, I am closest to...
- My siblings are...
- My father's trade is/was...
- My mother's trade is/was...
- My mother was consistently...
- My father was consistently...
- I'm like my mother in that I...
- I'm like my father in that I...
- I'm different from my mother in that I...
- I'm different from my father in that I...
- One of the best things one of my parents told me was...

OPINIONS/PREFERENCES:

- One of my biggest pet peeves is...
- My religious beliefs are...
- My political beliefs include...
- I vote (or don't vote) because...
- The government does too little for...
- The government has too much...
- I believe or don't believe in God because...
- The most overrated holiday is...
- The most annoying thing about today's technology is...

MEMORIES:

- As a child, my favorite game was...
- I'll never forget when I made the crazy choice to...
- The person I most miss in my life right now is...
- I got my first car when I was...

THIS GROUP:

- Some desires I have for this workshop are...
- Some fears or reservations I have about this workshop are...
- I am here today because...
- Learning these skills will help me...
- I'm in this course because...

CHAPTER 9

TOP NINE TIPS

1. When you meet a person, privately create wild, vibrant or unusual images to accompany their name.
2. When you re-meet someone whose name you have forgotten, reintroduce yourself. Nine times out of ten they will tell you their name too.
3. Repeat people's names over and over again, both in conversation and to yourself.
4. People are flattered when you remember their names. Learn to enjoy gratifying people in this way.
5. Give yourself manageable challenges. Start with committing to remember a person's name until the end of the conversation, until next week, until next year, etc.
6. Accept you won't remember everyone's

names all at once. Simply remember a few at a time.

7. Model learning names by reciting everybody's name at the end of a name game.

8. The brain uses up a fifth of all the oxygen we breath and a quarter of all the glucose we consume. Engage the entire body to get the brain utilized in creating new memories.

9. Make it fun!

ACKNOWLEDGMENTS

To my collaborators and protégés who have taught me so much and who are all now masters in their own right: Leilani Weis, Ray Chung, Sabine Parzer, and Gretchen Spiro.

Many people contributed ideas and name games for this book. Special thanks go to these wonderfully creative and generous teachers: Nancy Stark Smith, Scott Wells, Carol Swann, Anne Aronov, Brenton Cheng, Fernando Neder, Clover Catskill, Brando, Benno Vorhem, Rick Nodine, Keith Hennessey, Eckhard Mueller, Brad Stoller, and Peter Rosselli.

Thanks to Mick Diener and Kate Fowler for editing suggestions.

For manuscript midwifery skills, big thanks to John Johnson and Liza Keogh. And special thanks to Funda

Keonovich who helped guide the way to effortlessly write this book.

ABOUT THE AUTHOR

Martin Keogh has taught and performed the dance form 'Contact Improvisation' in over 32 countries spanning five continents. For his contribution to the development of the form he is a Fulbright Senior Specialist and listed in Who's Who in the World.

Keogh spent time traveling to monasteries in Japan and Korea and was the director of the Empty Gate Zen Center in Berkeley before discovering the world of dance. In the 1990s he founded 'The Dancing Ground,' an organization that produces conferences on gender, race and mythology.

Keogh attempts to teach and model that the beauty and reach of our questions, in the end, determine the beauty and reach of our lives.

ALSO BY MARTIN KEOGH

As Much Time as it Takes:

A Guide to Healthy Grieving

*This is a practical handbook for the bereaved
and their friends, how to live with grief, to express it
or not, how to find your natural way through. And
the quotations from Neruda, Machado, Dickinson
and others are beautifully chosen.*

--Coleman Barks author of The Essential Rumi

Hope Beneath Our Feet:

Restoring Our Place in the Natural World

*"This compelling and inspirational anthology raises
a chorus of voices in defense of the earth.* Hope
Beneath Our Feet *addresses the environmental
problems plaguing our planet and the myriad forms
of action each of us can take."*

--Leonardo DiCaprio, actor and activist

Dancing Deeper Still:

The Practice of Contact Improvisation

This compilation of 30 years of writings is meant to accompany and support dancer's investigation as they discover new pathways and dynamics in their dancing.

Visit martinkeogh.com